Dear Rabbi,

The Future of The Jews is Also in Your Hands

ISBN: 9781954713192

BH4 Publishing

This book is dedicated to the Jewish people.

This book is also dedicated to my parents, who insisted that I stay on the Jewish path with all its twists and turns, and to my wife, who joined me on this journey.

Motivation

I am far from perfect and have much to learn and improve upon. Who am I to provide a critical perspective on what I see all around me? I am a Jew, and I care about my Jewish brothers and sisters.

There are so few of us (less than 0.2% of the world's population), yet we have and continue to shape this world in so many ways.

This is my attempt to try and contribute to our common future. If this book helps improve the life of one Jewish family, then writing this book will have been worthwhile.

A positive impact on Jews can only positively impact the non-Jews in this world. And so, they too are on my mind as I write this book.

I have met many rabbis over the years. All had great intentions. All were good; some were brilliant.

Most knew their stuff. But to know the stuff is not enough.

We are losing Jews.

This book is not about left vs. right. It is not about reconstructionist vs. reform vs. conservative vs. modern orthodox vs. orthodox. I am not here to discuss who is on the right path and what is the right path.

If you are a Jew, you should read this book, and if you agree with the message, do something about it.

Do what?

I propose a specific high-level strategy in the later parts of this book. You could adopt this strategy partially or in its entirety and customize it to the need of your specific Jewish community.

I hereby take upon myself to fulfill the mitzvah, 'Love your fellow as yourself'

הֲרֵינִי מְקַבֵּל עָלַי מִצְוַת עֲשֵׂה שֶׁל וְאָהַבְתָּ לְרֵעֲךָ כָּמוֹךָ

Haraynee Mekabel Alai Mitzvat Asai Shel Ve'ahavta
Lerayacha kamocha.

Brief Table of Content

Table of Contents

Part I – Introduction

✡ DEAR RABBI, THIS BOOK IS NOT ONLY FOR YOU!
✡ DEAR RABBI AND ALL OTHER READERS OF THIS BOOK!
✡ DEAR RABBI, IF THE BOOK IS NOT ONLY FOR YOU, WHY DID I CALL IT "DEAR RABBI"?

Dear Rabbi, This Book is Not Only for You!

This book is for you, dear rabbi. It is also for members of your board of directors and all Jews that care – those that are members of your community/congregation, as well as Jews that are not affiliated with your or any other Jewish organization.

Every Jew who cares about the Jewish people's future should read this book, and more importantly, they should act.

Dear Rabbi and All Other Readers of This Book!

The Torah, the books that followed, and their interpretations by great rabbis since its writing bring a rich, meaningful, and powerful beauty to our lives.

There is nothing that will move me from who I am. You may choose to accept or reject my message in this book, but know that I come to you in peace.

Quoting from Number 6:24-26:

May the LORD bless thee and keep thee.

May the LORD shine his face toward thee, and be gracious unto thee.

May the Lord lift his face toward thee, and give thee peace.

יְבָרֶכְךָ יְהוָה ,וְיִשְׁמְרֶךָ

יָאֵר יְהוָה פָּנָיו אֵלֶיךָ ,וִיחֻנֶּךָּ

יִשָּׂא יְהוָה פָּנָיו אֵלֶיךָ ,וְיָשֵׂם לְךָ שָׁלוֹם

Yevarechecha Adonai, V'Yishmerecha
Ya'er Adonai Panav Eleycha, ViChoneka
Yisa Adonai Panav Eleycha, V'Yasem Lecha
Shalom

There are those Jews that have not been exposed to the beauty of the Torah as you have, or even to the lesser extent that I have experienced. For various reasons they are on their way out of the Jewish door.

Dear Rabbi, If the Book Is Not Only for You, Why Did I Call it "Dear Rabbi"?

You always had great questions, dear rabbi. This question is no exception. You are singled out for the simple reason that you are the chosen one! The one chosen to lead us. In this role, you have the ultimate responsibility among us, humans, to do it in the best way possible.

This book is here to remind you and all of us that you can and should do more. This book is to remind all of us who are not rabbis to help you lead us to do more.

Part II – It's All Good!

* DEAR RABBI, YOU DO SO MUCH!
* DEAR RABBI, YOU DO SO MUCH FOR YOUR CONGREGATION!
* DEAR RABBI, THE SYNAGOGUE LOOKS FANTASTIC!
* DEAR RABBI, THE SCHOOL IS FILLED WITH JEWISH CHILDREN!
* DEAR RABBI, YOU ARE AN AMAZING ASSET TO THE JEWISH UNIVERSITY / YESHIVA!
* DEAR RABBI, YOU ARE A POPULAR COMMUNITY LEADER!
* DEAR RABBI, YOU ARE A DILIGENT MASHGIACH!
* DEAR RABBI, THANK YOU FOR INVITING ME TO A SHABBAT MEAL AT YOUR SYNAGOGUE!
* DEAR RABBI, THANK YOU FOR INVITING ME TO A SHABBAT MEAL AT YOUR HOME!!!
* DEAR RABBI, WE NEED TO MAKE SURE YOU HAVE ENOUGH MONEY TO SUPPORT YOUR FAMILY!

Dear Rabbi, You Do So Much!

You work very hard, rabbi. You are earnest, and you are respected. You care. You love your people. You love the Torah. And, of course, you love G-d.

You pray three times a day.

You have a family to support and nurture. You may even want your children to follow in your footsteps and become Rabbis and Rebbetzins when they grow up.

Giving your family stability and security in this fast-changing world is not a simple task. I understand your family obligations.

I know that your family is your number one priority, which is how it should be.

I do appreciate all you are doing. Know that as a Jew, I am here to support you along the way.

Dear Rabbi, You Do So Much for Your Congregation!

If you have a congregation, you greet congregants and smile. You perform synagogue services. This may include daily, Shabbat, and holiday services. You perform ceremonies: bris, bar mitzvah, bat mitzvah, weddings. Mazal Tov! And then you also officiate funerals and visit the sick and the elderly. Thank you!

You meet with congregants. You listen to their stories, complaints, needs, and desires. You attend private events. When your large donors have an event and invite you... you go. I would too.

The study of the Torah and our other books is a lifelong journey. You study daily and diligently. You passionately teach your congregants – public sessions, small groups, one-on-one sessions.

Perhaps you write articles on Jewish topics for local newspapers or magazines. You may even write books. As your reputation grows, your congregation will attract more people on Shabbat to hear you speak. You have many children, and Jewish education and kosher food are not cheap. These activities can help pay for some of your family's needs.

Dear Rabbi, The Synagogue Looks Fantastic!

I remember when you started your career. The shul was in your home. Then it moved to a local storefront, and finally, after a successful fundraising campaign, there is a new shining building on main street. Did they teach fundraising in rabbinical school? Regardless, you are considered brilliant for making this happen!

Spacious facilities, kitchen, a hall or maybe four of them, and one or more sanctuaries! Wow! That stained glass is magnificent! Thank you, rabbi, for your ability to enlist donors behind this project. Looks amazing! A book should be written about your ability to convince people to donate so much money.

Dear Rabbi, The School is Filled with Jewish Children!

You built a reform school? The kids are learning Jewish Songs. They are learning about the Jewish holidays and much more!

You built a conservative school? Jewish boys and girls are also learning Hebrew and Torah and much more!

You built an orthodox school? Built a yeshiva for boys and another for girls? The kids also learn Hebrew, Rashi, Navi, Halacha, Chumash, Mishna, and Gemara. So much learning! You are teaching them Jewish law! No wonder there are so many Jewish lawyers!

Dear Rabbi, You Are an Amazing Asset to The Jewish University / Yeshiva!

Perhaps you do not have a congregation. You are a rabbi that teaches at a Jewish University or a Yeshiva! You are a scholar!

You spent your life studying and continue to do so. You dedicate your life to future generations of Jewish rabbis, cantors, leaders, administrators, and teachers for our Jewish communities. Thank you for doing what you do.

With all this learning, is it possible that your university or yeshiva forgets to convey something very important to your students? Anything is possible. Do consider creating a new course based on this book.

Dear Rabbi, You Are a Popular Community Leader!

Perhaps you are a community leader! You organize people and events. It is a mitzvah to get Jews out of their homes, allow them and their children to meet at events, and develop new friendships. This is a worthwhile endeavor!

Dear Rabbi, You Are a Diligent Mashgiach!

Perhaps you are a rabbi that supervises food service establishments, including slaughterhouses, food manufacturers, hotels, caterers, nursing homes, restaurants, butchers, grocery stores. You make sure that what some of us eat is Kosher! Thank you for doing this very special work.

Dear Rabbi, Thank You for Inviting Me to a Shabbat Meal at Your Synagogue!

Thanks for inviting me, rabbi. The synagogue looks great. The Jews dress so nice for Shabbat. Well... at least some do. And they are so polite... well... at least some are. There are those gum-chewing ladies... chewing with an open mouth. But let me not digress.

Your strategy will bring more people. Some may become members, and many will move on.

What is your goal with these meals, rabbi? To add more members to the shul? Bring more members to a united and strong Jewish people? Perhaps both?

Some Jews will come again and again to eat. You might make the big donors believe that you are popular, justifying continued donations. In doing so, are you acting in the best interests of the Jewish people or just executing the playbook?

Dear Rabbi, Thank You for Inviting Me to a Shabbat Meal at Your Home!!!

Friday night! That is very special indeed. My family, and perhaps another family or two, are invited for a meal in your home with your family. What a great opportunity to get to know each other better.

But rabbi, I am confused. Your company was marvelous, your family is wonderful, the food was great, and your home is warm and welcoming. But I am sorry to say something was missing! You did not ask me if I needed anything. You did not ask me if my family and I are ok. You did not ask if we needed help. You did not ask if everyone was healthy or if we needed some assistance with doctors in the community. You did not ask us if we are financially stable - able to sustain ourselves. Perhaps we need help to afford to eat kosher food and send our kids to a Jewish school. You did not ask us, nor did you offer help.

And I apologize. If these matters are not an appropriate conversation on Shabbat. You did not suggest a follow-up meeting to get to know us better after Shabbat either. You did not suggest to introduce us to others in the community. We may or may not need community help, but we all need community.

Dear Rabbi, We Need to Make Sure You Have Enough Money to Support Your Family!

You know, and I know of the many things that you do. Know that other Jews I know, and I, appreciate you and your efforts.

Know that each Jew that reads this book, that did not know, now knows about the many things that you do.

I know you have a mortgage to pay. I know we are no longer in the shtetel and that you want to live in a reasonably nice house that is spacious enough to accommodate your growing family. Nothing wrong with that.

Every Jew who knows you should give you what they can to support you and your family.

Part III – Oy Vey, It Could Be Better

- DEAR RABBI, LOOK AROUND, JEWS COME, AND JEWS GO
- DEAR RABBI, JEWS ARE INTERMARRYING ALL AROUND (WAIT – DON'T THROW AWAY THIS BOOK JUST YET, RABBI. I AM NOT GOING TO TAKE A PERSONAL POSITION ON INTERMARRIAGE HERE)
- DEAR RABBI, JEWS ARE WALKING AWAY
- DEAR RABBI, WHY ARE JEWS WALKING AWAY FROM BEING JEWS?
- DEAR RABBI, THE KGB KNEW WHERE EVERY JEW IN RUSSIA LIVED AND WHAT THEY DID
- DEAR RABBI, DO YOU OR YOUR STUDENTS WALK FROM OFFICE BUILDING TO OFFICE BUILDING EVERY FRIDAY, KNOCKING ON DOORS?
- DEAR RABBI, DO YOU CONDUCT OUTREACH TO JEWISH STUDENTS ON A CERTAIN UNIVERSITY CAMPUS? PERHAPS LEAD A HILLEL OR CHABAD HOUSE?
- DEAR RABBI, I AM NEW IN TOWN
- DEAR RABBI, I DO NOT HAVE A JOB TO SUSTAIN MY FAMILY AND ME

- ✿ DEAR RABBI, I HAVE A JOB, BUT IT DOES NOT PAY ENOUGH TO SUSTAIN MY FAMILY AND ME
- ✿ DEAR RABBI, I DO NOT HAVE ENOUGH BUSINESS TO SUSTAIN MY FAMILY AND ME
- ✿ DEAR RABBI? WHERE DID THEY GO?
- ✿ DEAR RABBI, I CAN'T FIND A JEWISH WIFE OR HUSBAND TO MARRY
- ✿ DEAR RABBI, I CAN'T AFFORD TO SEND MY KIDS TO JEWISH SCHOOL
- ✿ DEAR RABBI, I CAN'T AFFORD TO EAT KOSHER FOOD

Dear Rabbi, Look Around, Jews Come, and Jews Go

If everything is so fantastic, why am I writing this letter to you?

I noticed something odd. I noticed that people come once or a few times to shul but then they disappear. You have been doing this for a while, and maybe this is how it has always been. Maybe it is not so strange.

Why don't they come back? Is it something they didn't like? I think everything you do is brilliant. Why don't they?

But wait, there is that one thing I would have done differently if I were a rabbi.

What would I have done differently?

I would have looked around to see if there were new faces, approached each one, and asked them to reach out to me after the Shabbat or the holiday so we could schedule a time to meet, zoom, or talk over the phone. I would make it my goal to build more and more and more relationships with more and more of my people. Why do you not do that, rabbi?

Dear Rabbi, Jews Are Intermarrying All Around (Wait – don't throw away this book just yet, rabbi. I am not going to take a personal position on intermarriage here)

I will not express my opinion in this book. I will not criticize intermarriage or support it.

People are people. There are good and bad people in every group. And, I respect every person's decision to marry whoever they wish to marry.

I do wonder why Jews intermarry. There are only a few options:

- A Jew tried to find a Jewish partner but could not find one, expanded the search, and ended up finding a wonderful person that is not Jewish.
- A Jew who did not care who they would marry had no strong connection to other

Jews or the Jewish community. The Jew ended up finding a non-Jew, but this was not on purpose.

- A Jew did not want to find a Jewish partner. They did not have a good experience with other Jews and decided they only wanted to marry someone not Jewish.

If you are a reform rabbi, intermarriage is possibly a great way to bring more and more people into Judaism, you believe. If you are a conservative rabbi, you have learned to accept it. If you are orthodox, you cannot accept this.

Look at the facts. Look around in your reform or conservative synagogue or school. The building is not as filled with people on Shabbat as it was 10 or 20 years ago. The school has room to accept more students. More importantly, what will happen to this community in 10 or 20 years?

Yes, I agree with you – the Jewish population is not declining, but research shows that this is due to the fast growth of the orthodox community. With its high birth rates, the orthodox community is compensating for the decline of the reform and conservative communities. What should we do about this rabbi?

When a Jew marries a non-Jew, will the non-Jewish spouse embrace Judaism? To what level? Will they take their married partner and walk away from it, step by little step? There are other options, of course.

What will happen to the children when they grow up? Should we care?

Dear Rabbi, Jews Are Walking Away

Did you look at the PEW research? (see Appendix A)

Reform rabbi: More and more Jews are transitioning from reform to being non-affiliated

Conservative Rabbi: More and more Jews are transitioning from conservative to reform synagogue affiliation.

Orthodox Rabbi: Hardly any of those who leave reform or conservative affiliation join orthodox congregations.

I am sure you are not happy about this.

Dear Rabbi, Why Are Jews Walking Away from Being Jews?

Jews have been walking away from being Jews for a very long time. Among the more popular reasons we have:

- Can't afford to provide children with Jewish education
- Too much hate and no apparent benefit
- Can't afford kosher food
- Can't afford to rest on the Shabbat... need to work to support the family
- Don't know how to pray
- Too many rules
- Don't know anything about Judaism
- Don't want to be labeled

It does not matter why they are walking away! The question is, what will you do about it?

Dear Rabbi, The KGB Knew Where Every Jew in Russia Lived and What They Did

Do you know where every Jew in your neighborhood lives? Have you gone door to door to see who is behind each door with a mezuza? Do you know what their situation is? Are they doing fine? Do they need help?

Yes, rabbi, I know you are busy and possibly have problems with your family and don't have the time to get involved in everyone else's problems.

Dear Rabbi, Do You or Your Students Walk from Office Building to Office Building Every Friday, Knocking on Doors?

Do you or your students offer to put tefillin on men who work behind doors with a mezuzah affixed to them? Have you ever asked them if there is anything you can do to help them? Maybe they have a sick child and excessive medical expenses?

I am not implying that you should pay for anyone's medical expenses from your own pocket. I am implying something else. Do you see where I am going with this?

Dear Rabbi, Do You Conduct Outreach to Jewish Students on a Certain University Campus? Perhaps Lead a Hillel or Chabad House?

Do you keep in touch with the students once they graduate or refer them to another rabbi in their new location? Do you ask them how you can help them? Do you help them find employment? Do you help them start a business by connecting them with potential clients?

Do you know when they are scheduled to graduate? If they disappear before that scheduled time, do you follow up with them to see how they are progressing and if there is anything you can do to help them or their families?

Dear Rabbi, I Am New in Town

I know a Jew. He was younger then and new in town. Not this town rabbi, another one. He moved 2-3 times when he was younger, and the same thing happened again and again. Would you like to know what happened to him?

The young Jew went to various local synagogues and met with the rabbis. He had nice conversations each time. The rabbis told him about themselves and the congregations and encouraged him to come back on Shabbat to experience it. But there was one simple question they did not ask him. How can I help you, my child? How can I help you?

Later he got married and moved again. This time, he took his wife and met with several local rabbis, hoping that something new would happen. But it did not. No rabbi ever asked that young Jewish couple, how can I help the two of you? Do you need a job? Do you need help with starting a business? How is your business doing?

I am not implying that you should help young couples start a business, rabbi. I know you are busy. But rabbi... do you see where I am going with this?

Dear Rabbi, I Do Not Have a Job to Sustain My Family and Me

Dear rabbi, did anyone ever walk into your office and ask you to help them find a job? Probably not, you will say.

Speaking of unusual, have you ever met with a person for the first time and, out of the blue, asked them what they did for a living and if they needed help finding a job (if they were unemployed or underemployed)?

Imagine if you could help a person who needed a job find a job. Do you think they might appreciate you even more? Might talk about you with others? Might donate again and again?

Dear rabbi, I Have a Job, but It Does Not Pay Enough to Sustain My Family and Me

Have you ever asked Jews you meet for the first time if they earn enough to sustain themselves and their families? How memorable it would be if you asked them about this and offered to help get them to a place where they can sustain themselves and their families.

Dear Rabbi, I Do Not Have Enough Business to Sustain My Family and Me

Dear rabbi, have you ever surveyed all of your congregation and new people who come in the first time to see if they need a job or if they have a business – did you ask if the business is struggling and they need more clients? Did you ask them about how their business works so you can connect them with people that could help them grow their business?

Dear Rabbi? Where Did They Go?

Dear rabbi, when a congregant that donated one year did not donate the next year, have you ever followed up in person to speak with them and find out the reason for this? Did you ask them if they lost their job? If they need a job? And if they have a business, did you ask them how it is going with the business, and if they need more clients?

Dear Rabbi, I Cannot Find a Jewish Wife or Husband to Marry

Dear rabbi, are you systematically asking people in your community and guests that come in on their own if they are seeking to find a husband or wife? Are you helping match them up with others?

While this is not a Shabbat conversation, you can tell them on Shabbat that you would like to help and ask them to reach out to you over the next day or two to schedule a call, zoom, or an in-person meeting.

I know you are not a professional matchmaker. But maybe you can introduce them to one or two matchmakers in the community? If there is no matchmaker in your community... see if any of the ladies in the community want to get involved in such an important mission?

Dear Rabbi, I Cannot Afford to Send My Kids to Jewish School

Dear rabbi, you are the principal or the administrator of a Jewish day school, and a parent comes to you and tells you they can no longer afford to pay tuition.

Or a parent comes and asks for a reduction in tuition.

And of course, many parents apply each year and ask for tuition assistance.

You have managed to convince enough people in the community to set up a tuition assistance fund, and there is money to help a limited amount of students! (You do have significant abilities when it comes to convincing people).

But rabbi... did you ever offer those same parents help to find a job or help to find a better paying job? If they have a business, did you ever offer them help to connect them with potential clients? So, they no longer need that limited financial assistance.

And how about you, dear rabbi – you lead a congregation. How many families in your congregation send their children to public school? Do you ever ask them if they want to send their kids to a Jewish school?

Do you ask them if they send their children to public school because they cannot afford Jewish school tuition? Do you offer to help them resolve their financial difficulties by helping find them a (better) job or (more) clients for their business?

Dear Rabbi, I Cannot Afford to Eat Kosher Food

Kosher chicken, turkey, beef, cheese, and other items are so much more expensive than non-kosher items. Could it be that more people would eat Kosher foods if they could afford to do so?

Maybe they could use a better-paying job or more clients in their business.

Part IV – Jewish Charity

* THERE IS A PERCEPTION OUT THERE AMONG SOME NON-JEWS THAT JEWS ONLY HELP ONE ANOTHER AND THAT JEWS ONLY DO BUSINESS WITH ONE ANOTHER

* WHAT? JEWS DO NOT DONATE ENOUGH? THIS CAN NOT BE TRUE!

* DEAR RABBI, LET'S TALK ABOUT CHARITY - TZEDAKAH

* DEAR RABBI, SO MANY JEWS SUPPORT SO MANY NON-JEWISH CAUSES

* DEAR RABBI, SO MANY JEWS SUPPORT SO MANY JEWISH CAUSES

There is a Perception Out There Among Some Non-Jews That Jews Only Help One Another, And That Jews Only Do Business With One Another

Dear Rabbi, Jews are hated by some for always helping one another. Unfortunately, often we do not help one another. And when we do help other Jews, often we do not help in a meaningful way.

What? Jews Do Not Donate Enough? This Can Not Be True!

Yes, rabbi, Jews often donate so much. Jews are very generous people. They donate so much to Jewish causes and organizations. They donate so much to non-Jewish causes and organizations. Amazing. But this discussion is not about the level of donations.

The discussion is about Jews helping one another in ways beyond the donation of time and or money.

47

This is about also helping individuals and families get back on their feet or get started with their lives. It is different. Get someone a job or clients for their business. So, they do not need any more handouts from this or that organization. So that they will not need to beg for financial aid to send their kids to a Jewish school, so they will not end up rejected from Jewish school because they cannot afford it. So that they can take their rightful place in the community and, in turn, can help others.

Dear Rabbi, Let's Talk About Charity - Tzedakah

Each and every rabbi knows of Rabbi Moses Ben Maimon (Rambam), quotes the Rambam, studies the Rambam, and or teaches the Rambam's principles.

You know, and I know what the great Rambam (Maimonides) said about Charity. The highest level of charity is to help sustain a person before they become impoverished by helping them find employment or establishing them in business to make it unnecessary for them to become dependent on others.

See Appendix B for more information about Rambam's eight levels of charity.

Dear Rabbi, So Many Jews Support So Many Non-Jewish Causes

Many Jews support only non-Jewish causes: arts and culture, hospitals, poor people in one country, prosecuted people in another country. It is truly amazing how generous we are!

We all know some of these philanthropic Jews. Are you happy that they are not sharing with Jewish causes? Will you speak with them about it?

Of course, if they are also donating to you, you might want to keep quiet and not criticize them for not sharing more with other Jewish causes. I understand.

However, if they are not willing to donate to your causes, perhaps you should speak with them. Find out why they don't. Some bad experience with rabbis that did not care about them when they were younger and not so affluent? You cannot change what happened to them in the past. Still, you can let them know that a specific Jew in the community could benefit from a job or an additional client and provide them a compelling reason why it is important to help that Jew (perhaps they have a sick child). Ask them if you can approach them about specific personal assistance to another Jew!

You could tell them that you are no longer like those rabbis they met long ago who did not offer to help them.

Dear Rabbi, So Many Jews Support So Many Jewish Causes

There are many other Jews that support only Jewish causes or support both Jewish and non-Jewish causes. Over 4,000 great Jewish organizations support Jewish causes in the USA!

These organizations include:

- Addiction services

- Counseling and family services
- Clothing donation
- Employment training and resume writing
- Financial assistance and scholarships
- Food and nutrition assistance
- Holocaust services
- Immigrant assistance
- Incarcerated services
- Jewish federations
- Jewish community centers
- Jewish museums
- Jewish cultural centers
- Legal services
- Medical support services
- Mini loans
- Senior services
- Services for persons with disabilities

An outsider may look at all of this and be certain that with such a support network, no Jew is left behind. This, however, is far from reality.

The Jewish middle class is often left behind.

Part V – We Need Change!

* DEAR RABBI, WHO ARE THE MEMBERS OF YOUR BOARD OF DIRECTORS?
* DEAR RABBI, REMEMBER, WE ARE JEWS!
* DEAR RABBI, LET YOUR PEOPLE GO
* DEAR RABBI, IT STARTS AT THE TOP, WITH YOUR BOARD OF DIRECTORS
* DEAR RABBI, A FEW MORE WORDS ABOUT YOUR BOARD OF DIRECTORS
* DEAR RABBI, YOU KNOW, AND I KNOW ABOUT "KOL YISRAEL AREVIM ZEH BAZEH"

Dear Rabbi, Who Are the Members of Your Board of Directors?

Everyone knows that most if not all of your organization's board of directors are your major donors.

Everyone knows that they often set the direction for your congregation or other organization.

I suspect that sometimes you do not agree with this direction, but what choice do you have? You need their money.

You need money to eat, educate your children, build a synagogue, build a school, for programming, and more.

However, there is a cost to this strategy. Some of these wealthy donors live on a cloud and do not understand what is going on on the ground. They are not in touch with reality.

If one is affluent, forgive me for saying this, it doesn't make one intelligent. Being affluent does not make one knowledgeable. I do not want to list the tens of reasons why one can be rich but not intelligent or knowledgeable. These donors know their limitations, and so do we. They need to know that we appreciate their kindness, and this is more important than how intelligent or knowledgeable they are or are not.

We have all met a donor or two that donate just because they want to show off or be popular. Perhaps they donate to gain power over others or feel important (I hope they are reading this too. Regardless, I will send them a copy of this book, and so could you, rabbi... anonymously, of course).

Dear Rabbi, Remember, We Are Jews!

You know that we, the Jews, are as successful as it gets. The number of Nobel prizes we win (close to 25%), our contributions to arts, science, medicine, etc., the number of multinational companies we manage.

You know how creative we are. Look around you; in your shul, we are your congregation's members, and we are creative. Look around you, in your school, we are the parents, and many of us are creative.

Working together, we can be more creative. But we are not working together. And if we are, often it is not done productively. And we know why this is so...

Dear Rabbi, Let Your People Go

We can turn Jewish continuity into a great success! But we need you to lead the way. We need you to facilitate. You need to let your people go - to help one another and help others. You need to constantly remind us of the virtue of performing mitzvot (good deeds) for their own sake.

This is not about some one-time event. This is about a new way of community living and providing a new sense of belonging.

Dear Rabbi, It Starts at The Top, With Your Board of Directors

You are surrounded by your more affluent donors. They support you, your family, your children's education. You need them.

These affluent donors are good people for the things they do. They should be commended for their support. They need to be recognized at each possible opportunity for their efforts if recognition is what they seek.

But is it possible that being wealthy and having good intentions is not enough? Is it possible that your wealthy donors need some direction? And I know you know this. However, you are probably reluctant to approach them. Most likely, you are afraid to shake the tree that is giving you beautiful apples.

Well, rabbi, I think it is time for you to shake that tree and ask the wealthy donors for more.

What more? Not for more money!

They are affluent, which means they likely have businesses. You can motivate them to help Jews in the community and Jews interested in becoming part of the community. These affluent Jews can hire community members to work for them. These affluent

Jews can become clients of Jews with struggling or startup businesses!

Dear Rabbi, A Few More Words About Your Board of Directors

We need to start looking at the shul as our second home. We need to build upon an earlier model of the European shtetl where life was based in the home as well as the synagogue.

You may need to develop new leaders or a new sense of purpose for your present leaders. Wait, don't close the book thinking there is no way you can accomplish this. You can.

How?

Keep the existing board of directors! They want and need to feel and appear important. They must stand at the podium and speak each Shabbat at the shul, etc. The walls must adorn their names.

But you should, with their blessing, form a second board of directors. A WORKING board of directors. The criteria to join this board should not be based on financial contributions but rather willingness to contribute time to building a more vibrant and more meaningful Jewish community that will support your goals and promote Jewish continuity.

These new people should be passionate about connecting people:

- Connecting individuals that need jobs to individuals that have jobs to give
- Connecting individuals that have startups or businesses that are struggling to proven and successful business leaders in the community
- Connecting Jewish men that want to find Jewish women to marry with possible matches, and vice versa
- Connecting families on financial aid to people that have jobs or to potential clients
- Check on the well-being of each congregant and let them know that they matter on an ongoing basis. If there is an issue, bring it to the attention of the members of the working board of directors, and place the issue on the board's formal agenda.

Dear Rabbi, You Know, and I Know About "Kol Yisrael Arevim Zeh Bazeh"

All of Israel Are Responsible for One Another

כל ישראל ערבים זה בזה

Kol Yisrael Arevim Zeh Bazeh

We all know that all of Israel are responsible for each other. This statement lays the foundation of communal responsibility in Jewish law. If one Jew sees another Jew on the verge of sinning, they are obligated to step in and help. This implies an obligation for each Jew to ensure that other Jews have their basic needs for food, clothing, shelter, and Jewish education for their children taken care of. Simply by being a Jew, one is responsible for the well-being of other Jews and vice versa.

Part VI – Strategy for Change

* WHAT NEXT?
* ENHANCED ORGANIZATIONAL GOALS
* ENHANCED ORGANIZATIONAL STRUCTURE
* MODIFIED APPROACH TOWARDS YOUR COMMUNITY
* MODIFIED APPROACH TOWARDS VISITORS

What Next?

To keep more and more Jews from walking away, and to bring more and more Jews back, we need to look at four things:

- Enhanced organizational goals
- Organizational structure enhancement in support of enhanced organizational goals
- Modified approach towards your community
- Modified approach toward visitors

Let's look at these four in greater detail next, dear rabbi.

Enhanced Organizational Goals

I am not asking you to change your organization's goals. But rather you could consider adding a few goals:

Goal 1: Tzedakah Awareness - Make the community aware of the highest level of Tzedakah and let them know that they too have a responsibility. Make this an ongoing effort. You could post posters on the walls, talk about Tzedakah, each Shabbat and holidays, etc.

Goal 2: Community Resources - Identify available community resources willing to help others and what they can contribute (members that may be able to hire people, help them find jobs, help with medical issues, help find a match).

Goal 3: Jobs - Identify who cannot support their families and match them with those that can assist with a job.

Goal 4: Business - Identify those with a struggling or startup business, and match them with those that might be able to become their clients.

Goal 5: Shidduch - Identify who needs a match and connect them with people in the community that can assist them in finding a husband or wife.

Goal 6: Medical Assistance - Identify people who have medical issues in their families and connect them to others that may be able to help.

Enhanced Organizational Structure

Keep your top donors and anyone else you have on your board of directors.

Create a new committee (you can call it the Tzedakah Committee, or the Tzedakah Board of Directors). This new group will comprise of caring and talented volunteers from the community.

They will play a key role in connecting those in need with those who can help them get (back) on their feet.

Modified Approach Towards Your Community

You need to constantly convey to your community (or existing network) the message that we all are responsible for helping one another.

You need to constantly convey the message that the highest level of Tzedakah/charity is helping those in need become independent of others.

Modified Approach Towards Visitors

Change should start with you! You need to talk to people individually, in groups, and as a community about the ultimate Tzedakah. This cannot be a one-time discussion but a lifelong process that never ends.

The community needs to be welcoming to visitors. Either you or an assigned community member should offer to follow-up with them (if the visitor comes on Shabbat or another holiday, and you cannot write, encourage the visitor to follow up with you immediately after the Shabbat or another holiday to learn more about them). You will then use that follow-up meeting to identify ways in which you could direct them to your community's resources so that help can be provided. You can then follow up with them and your committee periodically to make sure progress is made and so that they can see that they matter.

In the event the visitor has no issues, you should find out if they could offer help to members of the community (perhaps the visitor is a business owner and can hire community members or conduct business with them).

Part VII – Epilogue

- ✡ DEAR RABBI, YOUR TURN TO WRITE
- ✡ DEAR RABBI, THANK YOU FOR UNDERSTANDING WHY YOU WERE SINGLED OUT IN THIS BOOK!

Dear Rabbi, Your Turn to Write

Do you write sermons? Do you write articles for your congregation or beyond? Do you write books? Great.

How about writing about the issues I raised in this book and boldly speaking about creating and maintaining community. Never stop writing about this. Never stop speaking about this.

Wherever there is a discussion about Tzedakah and Jewish giving, there should be a portion dedicated to the Tzedakah / giving discussed in this book. About the need for Jews to help one another find a job, start and grow a business. Help each other become independent, so we do not have to ask for financial assistance to have our kids study in Jewish schools. So that we do not have to send them to non-Jewish religious schools or public schools just because we cannot afford Jewish education for them.

I believe that if today's Jews learn and participate in community building and make personal connections, they will be much more likely to embrace Jewish values.

Dear Rabbi, Thank You for Understanding Why You Were Singled Out in This Book!

You know why you were chosen, dear rabbi.

Yes, each Jew has a responsibility to help another Jew.

Yes, each Jew that can offer a job to another Jew that needs one should do so. Yes, each member of the board of directors should consider adjusting their approach in support of all that we have discussed here.

But you, rabbi…, chose to be one of our leaders.

Or maybe, you did not choose but were chosen to be.

Either way, you have the highest level of responsibility (amongst us humans), and thus this book was DEDICATED to you.

Lead your congregations back to Jewish roots and community values.

May G-d bless you and guard you.

May G-d shine His countenance upon you and be gracious to you.

May G-d turn His countenance toward you and grant you peace. (Numbers 6:24-26)

יְבָרֶכְךָ יהוה ,וְיִשְׁמְרֶךָ

יָאֵר יהוה פָּנָיו אֵלֶיךָ ,וִיחֻנֶּךָ

יִשָּׂא יהוה פָּנָיו אֵלֶיךָ ,וְיָשֵׂם קָ שָׁלוֹם

Yivarechecha Adonai viyishmirecha

Ya'er Adonai panav elecha veechuneka

Yeesa Adonai panav elecha viyasem lecha shalom

If you have any ideas for improvement of this book, please email me at david@GeffenRealEstate.com or text me at 310-433-0694

If you enjoyed this book, please consider posting a review. Even if it's only a few sentences, it would be a huge help. Thank you.

Appendix A – Relevant Research

Per PEW research (www.PewResearch.org):

"Younger Jews are more likely than older Jews to identify as Orthodox and more likely to say they do not belong to any particular branch of Judaism. Jews under 30 appear to be taking divergent paths – one steeped in traditional religious observance, the other involving little or no religious engagement. Some 17% of U.S. Jews ages 18 to 29 say they are Orthodox, compared with 3% of Jews ages 65 and older. At the same time, 41% of young Jewish adults do not identify with any particular branch of American Judaism. Most of the people in this category are "Jews of no religion" – they describe their religion as atheist, agnostic or nothing in particular, though they all have a Jewish parent or were raised Jewish and still identify as Jewish culturally, ethnically or because of their family background.

Meanwhile, the Reform and Conservative movements, American Judaism's largest branches, seem to be losing ground with younger generations. About four-in-ten Jews ages 18 to 29 identify as

Reform (29%) or Conservative (8%), compared with seven-in-ten Jews who are 65 and older (44% Reform, 25% Conservative)."

Among younger Jewish adults, 17% identify as Orthodox and 41% don't identify with any branch

% of U.S. Jews who are ...

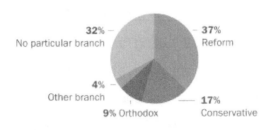

	Orthodox	Conservative	Reform	No particular branch	Other branch
Age 18-29	17%	8%	29%	41%	5%
30-49	11	11	37	36	4
50-64	7	22	35	30	5
65+	3	25	44	22	4

Note: Those who did not answer are not shown. Figures include both Jews by religion and Jews of no religion. Virtually all Orthodox Jews (99%) and Conservative Jews (99%) in the survey are Jews by religion, as are 88% of Reform Jews. Most Jews who are unaffiliated with a branch are Jews of no religion (65%).
Source: Survey conducted Nov. 19, 2019-June 3, 2020, among U.S. adults.
"Jewish Americans in 2020"

"About four-in-ten married Jews (42%) have a non-Jewish spouse, but intermarriage rates differ within subgroups. For example, intermarriage is almost nonexistent among married Orthodox Jews (2%), while nearly half of all non-Orthodox Jews who are married say their spouse is not Jewish (47%). Intermarriage is more common among those who have married in recent years: Among Jewish respondents who got married since the beginning of 2010, 61% have a non-Jewish spouse, compared with 18% of Jews who got married before 1980. Intermarriage also is more common among Jews who are themselves the offspring of intermarried parents: Among married Jews who say they have one Jewish parent, 82% have a non-Jewish spouse, compared with 34% of those who report that both of their parents were Jewish."

See for more information:

https://www.pewresearch.org/fact-tank/2021/05/11/10-key-findings-about-jewish-americans/

"Within Judaism, denominational switching has led to the largest net losses for the Conservative movement, which, in the 1950s and 1960s, was the largest branch of American Jewry.

For every person who has joined Conservative Judaism, about three have left the denomination."

For every person who has joined Conservative Judaism, about three have left the denomination

Among U.S. adults who are Jewish today or who were raised as Jews by religion or Jews of no religion ...

	Childhood denomination/ Jewish status	Left	Joined	Current denomination/ Jewish status
Orthodox Judaism	10%	3%	1%	8%
Conservative Judaism	25	14	5	15
Reform Judaism	28	10	16	33
No denomination	17	7	19	29

Note: The far left and far right columns do not add to 100% because respondents who were not raised Jewish but currently identify as Jewish or respondents who were raised Jewish but are not currently Jewish are not shown. Jews who identify with smaller denominations (such as Reconstructionist Judaism and Humanistic Judaism) and Jews who did not answer the question about their branch identification during childhood or at present are also not shown.
Source: Survey conducted Nov. 19, 2019-June 3, 2020, among U.S. adults.
"Jewish Americans in 2020"

PEW RESEARCH CENTER

"In the new survey, a quarter of adults who are currently Jewish or were raised that way say they were brought up in Conservative Judaism, while 15% identify as Conservative Jews today. For every person who has joined Conservative Judaism, nearly three people who were raised in the Conservative movement have left it.

By contrast, Reform Judaism – now the largest American Jewish denomination – has experienced a net gain due to religious switching; 28% of current or former U.S. Jews say they were raised as Reform Jews, while 33% currently identify with the Reform movement.

Jews with no denominational affiliation also have experienced a net gain. About one-in-six current or former U.S. Jews (17%) say they were raised in no particular branch of Judaism, while 29% currently identify with no branch. For every person who has left this group (either to join another branch or to leave Judaism altogether), nearly three people have joined the ranks of U.S. Jews who do not affiliate with any particular Jewish denomination.

Meanwhile, one-in-ten current or former U.S. Jews say they were raised in Orthodox Judaism, and 8% currently identify as Orthodox. Despite this small net loss from denominational switching, some social scientists project that the Orthodox share of the Jewish population is likely to increase in the future, because Orthodox Jews are younger and have a higher fertility rate than non-Orthodox Jews, on average.

Orthodox and Reform Judaism have the highest retention rates

Another way of examining changes in denominational affiliation is to calculate retention rates: Among adults who were raised in a given branch of Judaism, what percentage still identify with that branch today? And where did the rest go?"

About two-thirds of adults raised as Orthodox or Reform Jews still identify with those branches

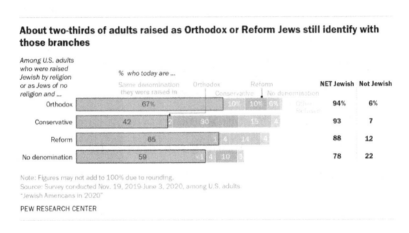

Note: Figures may not add to 100% due to rounding.
Source: Survey conducted Nov. 19, 2019-June 3, 2020, among U.S. adults
"Jewish Americans in 2020"

PEW RESEARCH CENTER

"Orthodox and Reform Judaism have the highest retention rates of the three major branches. Two-thirds of adults who were raised as Orthodox (67%) and Reform Jews (65%) still identify with those branches, respectively. The retention rate of Conservative Judaism is lower: About four-in-ten people raised as Conservative Jews (42%) continue to identify with Conservative Judaism as adults.

Adults who no longer identify with their childhood denomination tend to have moved in the direction of less traditional, more theologically liberal forms of Judaism – or to have left Judaism altogether – rather than in the direction of more traditional branches. For example, 57% of people raised within Conservative Judaism now either identify with Reform Judaism (30%), don't identify with any particular branch of Judaism (15%) or are no longer Jewish (7%), while only 2% now identify with Orthodox Judaism.

Many Reform Jews were raised in more traditional branches. Yet another way of looking at denominational switching is to calculate "accession rates": Among adults who identify with a given branch of Judaism today, what percentage were not raised in that branch, and where did they come from?"

A quarter of Reform Jews were raised in either Conservative or Orthodox Judaism

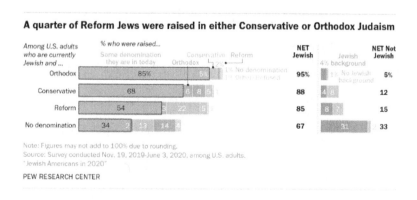

Note: Figures may not add to 100% due to rounding.
Source: Survey conducted Nov. 19, 2019-June 3, 2020, among U.S. adults.
"Jewish Americans in 2020"

PEW RESEARCH CENTER

"Most Orthodox Jewish adults (85%) and Conservative Jewish adults (68%) were raised in their current denomination. In other words, just 15% of today's Orthodox Jews came from outside Orthodoxy, including 5% who were raised as Conservative and 2% who were raised as Reform. Meanwhile, about a third of today's Conservative Jews (32%) were not raised in that movement, including 6% who were brought up as Orthodox and 8% who were raised as Reform.

The Reform movement has a somewhat higher accession rate. Nearly half (46%) of today's Reform Jews have come from outside the Reform movement. A quarter of today's Reform Jews were raised as either Conservative (22%) or Orthodox (3%).

The group with the highest accession rate, however, is Jews with no denominational affiliation. Two-thirds (66%) of adults in this category were raised in other groups, including 13% who were raised as Conservative Jews, 14% who were raised as Reform Jews and 33% who say they were not raised as Jewish at all (though most say they had a Jewish parent).

A relatively small proportion of respondents identify as Jewish today but say they did not have a

Jewish parent and were not raised Jewish in any way. This group makes up 8% of adult Conservative Jews, 7% of Reform Jews, 2% of Jews with no denominational affiliation and 1% of Orthodox Jews. The survey did not ask whether they have gone through a formal Jewish conversion."

See for more information:

https://www.pewresearch.org/fact-tank/2021/06/22/denominational-switching-among-u-s-jews-reform-judaism-has-gained-conservative-judaism-has-lost/

Appendix B – Maimonides (Rambam) Says

Rabbi Moses Ben Maimon (Rambam) teaches us that there are eight levels of Tzedakah (charity). They are (from the least to the most proper):

- Level 8 - Donating grudgingly.
- Level 7 - Giving less than one should give but doing so cheerfully.
- Level 6 - Giving directly to the poor when asked.
- Level 5 - Giving directly to the poor without being asked.
- Level 4 – When the recipient knows the donor's identity, but the donor does not know the recipient's identity
- Level 3 – When the donor knows the recipient's identity, but the recipient does not know the donor's identity.
- Level 2 – The donor and recipient are unknown to each other.
- Level 1 – Sustaining a person before they become impoverished, via any of:

- substantial gift
- substantial loan
- helping them find employment
- helping them get established in business

so that they don't need to become dependent on others.

It is ironic that in major cities throughout the world, there are schools in his name, yet the teaching of his perspective on Charity is not being effectively instilled in us. So please, dear Rabbi, remember that the future of the Jewish people is also in your hands...

If you have any ideas for improvement of this book please email me at david@GeffenRealEstate.com or text me at 310-433-0694

If you enjoyed this book, please consider posting a review. Even if it's only a few sentences, it would be a huge help. Thank you.